YOUR KNOWLEDGE HAS VALUE

Findley Penn-Hughes

A Fool's Paradise? Ethnicity, Military and Prospects for Democratisation in Myanmar

GRIN Verlag

Bibliografische Information der Deutschen Nationalbibliothek:

Die Deutsche Bibliothek verzeichnet diese Publikation in der Deutschen National-bibliografie; detaillierte bibliografische Daten sind im Internet über http://dnb.d-nb.de/ abrufbar.

Imprint:

Copyright © 2013 GRIN Verlag GmbH
Druck und Bindung: Books on Demand GmbH, Norderstedt Germany
ISBN: 978-3-656-76449-6

This book at GRIN:

http://www.grin.com/en/e-book/280409/a-fool-s-paradise-ethnicity-military-and-prospects-for-democratisation

GRIN - Your knowledge has value

Der GRIN Verlag publiziert seit 1998 wissenschaftliche Arbeiten von Studenten, Hochschullehrern und anderen Akademikern als eBook und gedrucktes Buch. Die Verlagswebsite www.grin.com ist die ideale Plattform zur Veröffentlichung von Hausarbeiten, Abschlussarbeiten, wissenschaftlichen Aufsätzen, Dissertationen und Fachbüchern.

Visit us on the internet:

http://www.grin.com/

http://www.facebook.com/grincom

http://www.twitter.com/grin_com

Table of Content

Glossary

Amyotha Hluttaw	Nationalities Legislative Assembly
Pyihtaungsu Hluttaw	Union Legislative Assembly; two houses of 2008 Constitution sitting together.
Sangha	Collective term for the Buddhist Monks
Tatmadaw	Military or armed forces

Honourifics

Bogyoke	Commander/General/Leader
Daw	Ms. (Used for mature women or those in a senior position)
Ko	Brother (older, used for men of a similar age)
Muang	Brother (younger, often used as part of a given name)
U	Mr. (Used for mature men or those in a senior position)

Abbreviations

ASEAN	Association of South East Asian Nations
AFPFL	Anti-Fascist People's League
BSPP	Burma Socialist Program Party
ENC	Ethnic Nationalities Council
KIA	Kachin Independence Army
KIO	Kachin Independence Organisation
NED	National Endowment for Democracy
NLD	National League for Democracy
SEA	Southeast Asia
SLORC	State Law and Order Restoration Council
SNLD	Shan Nationalities League for Democracy
SPDC	State Peace and Development Council
UNDP	Union National Democracy Party
USDA	Union Solidarity and Development Association
USDP	Union Solidarity and Development Party

Major Ethnic Groups of Myanmar

Figure 1

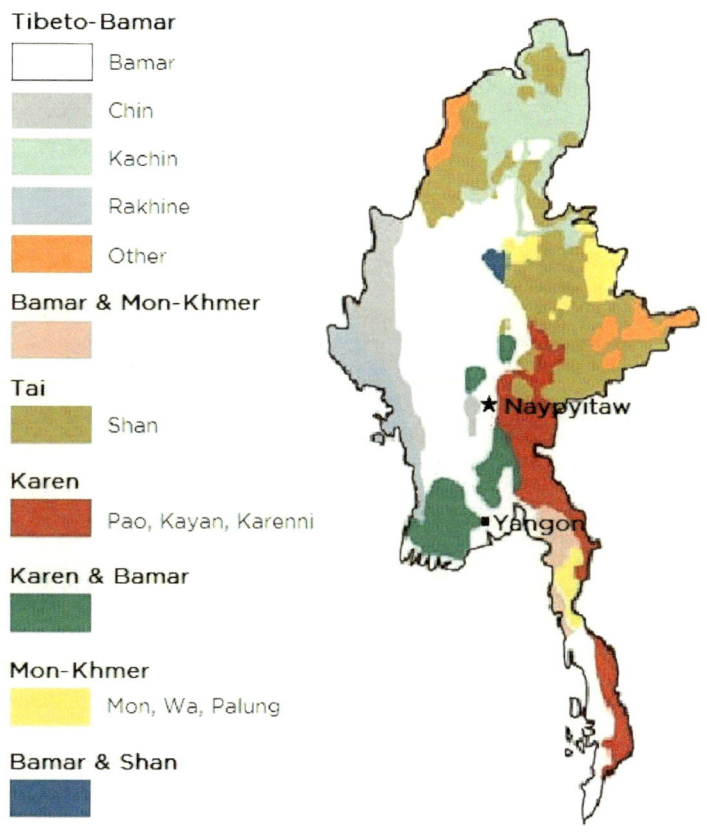

Source: M. J. Smith, *Burma: Insurgency and the Politics of Ethnicity* (London: Zed Book Ltd, 1991) p. xix

Terminology

Burmese names

The Burmese do not employ patrilineal or matrilineal naming systems, and as such do not use surnames or family names. For this reason when naming someone the whole name is used. Thus neither Ms. Aung Sang nor Ms. Suu Kyi is correct - Aung Sang Suu Kyi is the only correct formulation. For this reason, Burmese names are listed in full throughout.

A complex system of honourifics that can infer status, age or position, are used in the Burmese language. The most common of these are listed in the glossary. Daw, as in Daw Aung Sang Suu Kyi, is commonly used to denote seniority, either in age or position, in women. Similarly, U (occasionally transliterated Oo) is used for men, as in U Thant. Occasionally these honourifics form part of a given name and where this is the case they are listed as such in full[1].

Burma or Myanmar?

Although the Burmese language name of the country has included 'Myanmar' since independence in 1948, the country officially held the English name 'Burma' until the regime changed it to 'Myanmar' 1989. It is important to note, however that the country name has always been 'Myanmar' in Burmese. The NLD, international news agencies and much of the international community continue to use 'Burma' to this day; but it is the subject of much controversy. Through the same period, the regime also began changing colonial era names to locally transliterated ones, as in the case of Rangoon to Yangon and others.

The word 'Burma' is derived from the spoken form of the name in the dialect of the dominant ethnic group, the Bamar. This has led some to dismiss it as a product of the dominance of the majority ethnic group. For reasons of clarity and to provide congruence with the Burmese language transliteration of the name, this paper will use the name 'Myanmar' and modern transliterations of city and place names throughout. The term Burmese will be used to denote the people or the language, as is convention[2].

---

[1] For more on Burmese names see: Mi Mi Khiang, "Burmese Names: A guide," *The Atlantic* 1958, Accessed: 7/1/2013.

[2] For more on this issue see: Lowell Dittmer, "Burma vs. Myanmar: What's in a Name?," *Asian Survey* 48, no. 6 (2008).

I.   Introduction

1.1.   Contextualising Myanmar

Myanmar's strategic and political influence in the region throughout its history has been instrumental in the formation of the modern state. The classical Kingdom of Bagan commanded authority over an area stretching across Irrawaddy Delta, the Upper Mekong and into present day India and Thailand[3]. This cultural and political power was supported in turn by military might, culminating in the sacking of Ayutthaya in 1569[4], in modern day Thailand, and marking the beginning of centuries of dominance over Siam and the region[5]. By the early colonial period Myanmar was the 'rice basket' of Asia, the world's largest exporter of rice[6] with the world's busiest immigrant port, Yangon, as its capital[7]. Military rule following independence from Ne Win's era to the dictatorships' of Than Shwe and Thein Sein were as oppressive as they were resilient. By the mid 2000s, scholars were rewriting the 'rule books' in an attempt to explain the continued existence of military rule; they rationalised this resistance through an appreciation of a complex interplay of cultural, religious and historical factors. Political developments today are trumpeted a sign that Myanmar has begun an inevitable transition to full civilian control and democracy.

The almost continual struggle to establish a Bamar nation across the centuries still informs political decision making in Myanmar today. The dynastic struggles of Bagan era; the annexation of Myanmar as part of British India for over 100 years; the subsequent struggle for self-determination; Japanese occupation during WWII; the ensuing civil war and ethnic

---

[3] R.H. Taylor, *The State in Myanmar* (London: C Hurst & Co Publishers Ltd, 2009). xxvi.
[4] An event still remembered and commemorated in Thailand today. A popular Thai film about the event, *Sukhothai*, is indicative of the cultural residue the Thais still possess today about the dominance of the Burmese.
[5] B. J. Terwiel, *Thailand's Political History: From the 13th Century to Recent Times* (Bangkok: River Books, 2011). 22.
[6] Taylor, *The State in Myanmar*: 141.
[7] Thant Myint-U, *Where China Meets India: Burma and the New Crossroads of Asia* (London: Faber & Faber, 2011). 18.

conflicts, and more recently the neo-colonial ambitions of China and the West in their competition over resources.

Geographically Myanmar sits at the "new crossroads of Asia"[8], a geo-politically vital intersection between a rising India and China on one side, and continental Southeast Asia (SEA) on the other. Its borders with China, Laos and Thailand are characterised by mountainous, largely uninhabitable regions. The exploitation by smugglers, drug-traffickers and ethnic insurgencies has throughout history both challenged and bolstered state authority. The bitter historical experience of these regions as the launching point for foreign invasion only serves to underpin their importance in the eyes of the state[9].

The outlying zones form a horseshoe shape around the Bamar majority heartland that sits on the central and Irrawaddy delta regions. The multiethnic, multicultural areas largely reflect the geographical divisions, with the ethnic minority groups as the principal inhabitants of the periphery. A growing perception of Bamar majority dominance is bolstered by the isolation and the increased urbanisation of these lowland areas[10]. Newer claims by Chinese and Western firms to the large reserves of natural resources have sparked accusations of acquiescence to foreign interests at the expense of the ethnic minorities.[11]

1.2.   A 'Burmese Spring': The New Light of Myanmar?

State and military power have been formally fused in Myanmar since the military coup of 1962. Colonial and pre-colonial experiences prior to this had ensured the creation of a national narrative that emphasised unity and the survival of the regime above all else. This led to the slow infiltration of military rule in the years following independence in 1948 and ultimately to the decades of authoritarian rule and economic mismanagement, exacerbated

---

[8] Ibid.

[9] Taylor, *The State in Myanmar*: 13.

[10] M. Than, "Myanmar: Preoccupation with Regime Survival, National Unity and Stability," in *Asian Security Practice: Material and Ideational Influences*, ed. M. Alagappa (Palo Alto: Stanford University Press, 1998), 392.

[11] Brian McCartan, "Land grabbing as big business in Myanmar," *Asia Times Online*, 8/03/2013, http://www.atimes.com/atimes/Southeast_Asia/SEA-01-080313.html, (Accessed: 10/03/2013.)

by economic sanctions. As the rest of the region began its post-colonial transition towards democracy and prosperity, brutal military crackdowns and reprisals following populist uprisings in 1988 and 2007 seemed only to confirm Myanmar's resilience. Following the suppression of the 2007 uprising, it appeared that the hold of the military junta was absolute and intransigent.

The announcement in 2008 by the ruling State Peace and Development Council (SPDC) of wide-ranging reforms as part of the 'roadmap to democracy' thus represented the greatest hope of democratic reform for half a century. Following the enactment of constitutional reforms and trumpeted elections in 2010, the state now represents an ostensibly democratic, constitutional system. Throughout early 2011 the newly formed 'civilian' government released over 700 political prisoners, oversaw a relaxation of media censorship and legalised the right to unionisation in conjunction with a re-emergence of opposition politics. President, formally General, Thein Sein met with Aung Sang Suu Kyi (ASSK), the leader of the main opposition, the NLD, in August 2011 marking a watershed moment in state engagement with the opposition. While large portions of the press hailed this as an immediate success, scholars were divided. Some have argued that the state is incapable of producing the policy outcomes it claims to pursue[12] while others see it as the first critical step in the transition towards, and consolidation of, democracy[13]. The regime's suspension of the Chinese-backed Myitsone dam in the face of public pressure is cited as a pivotal point in the regime's response to the opposition and its relationship with civil society groups[14]. Observers note that the emergence of these groups and the presence of a viable opposition as deciding factors in the political trajectory, cautiously optimistic in an eventual democratic outcome.

---

[12] Sean Turnell, "Myanmar in 2011," *Asian Survey* 52, no. 1 (2012).
[13] Muang Zarni, "An Insider View of Reconciliation," in *Myanmar/Burma: Inside Challenges, Outside Interests*, ed. L. Rieffel (Washington, D.C.: Brookings Institution Press, 2010); Morten B Pedersen, "The Politics of Burma's "Democratic" Transition," *Critical Asian Studies* 43, no. 1 (2011).
[14]"Burma dam: Work halted on divisive Myitsone project," *BBC News*, Accessed: 5/1/2013, http://www.bbc.co.uk/news/world-asia-pacific-15121801, (Accessed: 5/1/2013.)

1.3.   Establishing the military-ethnic dynamic

What these accounts lack is an explanation of the military framework and decision making process, and its role in civil-military relations in what is an ostensibly a civilian government. Although the new Constitution provides safeguards for civilian autonomy, it simultaneously guarantees military veto power in the *Hluttaw* legislature. Whilst some have pointed to the relative inactivity of the military in exercising these powers as evidence of their acquiescence to politics[15], this paper will argue it points to broader concerns on the part of the military elites; concerns over territorial integrity and the centralisation of Myanmar.

Despite the regime singing peace agreements with most the most of the armed ethnic insurgencies in the 1990s, many conflicts are still ongoing. The latest Burmese census from 1983 showed that ethnic Bamars constituted 69 percent of the population; Shan, Karen, Arakanese, Mon and Kachin groups made up 20 percent with the remainder formed of over a hundred smaller language groups[16]; representing an equally diverse number of political aims and degrees of political participation. The recent reform process has seen renewed calls for autonomy and a re-emergence of armed incidents in many of these areas. Despite recently signed ceasefires and its more general withdrawal from politics, the military continues to operate unilaterally in contravention of these agreements[17]. An analysis of the military framework will show how the development of military's emphasis on state centralisation and integrity has led to its subsequent adoption of ethnic conflict as its 'reserved domain'.

The military and ethnic movements in Myanmar thus find their definition in opposition to one another, with the military locating its *raison d'être* in the suppression of these ethnic movements. This paper will argue that the current reform process, far from being a sign of

---

[15] Mary Callahan, "The Generals Loosen Their Grip," *Journal of Democracy* 23, no. 4 (2012).

[16] Ardeth Maung Thawnghmung, "Beyond armed resistance: ethnonational politics in Burma (Myanmar)," in *Policy Studies* (Honolulu: East-West Center, 2011), 3

[17] Al Jazeera, "Kachin rebels say Myanmar ignoring ceasefire," *Al Jazeera*, 21/2/2013, Accessed: 25/2/2013, http://www.aljazeera.com/news/asia-pacific/2013/01/20131212566922246.html, (Accessed: 26/2/2013.)

an irreversible trajectory towards democracy, is a choreographed, long-term policy adopted by the military to perpetuate its position in politics. The theoretical framework of exogenous and endogenous factors behind military withdrawal will demonstrate how the internal structure of the *Tatmadaw* impacts its political decision making. The cultural and historical factors behind this predispose it to consider the ethnic question as the primary purpose for its existence. Consequently, despite progress towards democratisation and largely favourable conditions to withdrawal, the military still occupies a position as the primary arbiter of power, through an appeal to unity. By simultaneously maintaining this political power, and failing to tackle the ethnic question outside of the military sphere, the Tatmadaw creates a self-perpetuating paradigm. The constitutionalistion of a political system which shuts down meaningful opposition only adds to this. By seeing itself as the solution to the ethnic question, when it is, in fact, the cause, the military position in politics fatally undermines Myanmar's prospects for democracy.

1.4. Problems of research methodology

The problems encountered when researching Myanmar are similar to those encountered in any closed and developing state. Statistics and raw data are hard to come by, either on poorly maintained government websites or physical archives. Despite some moves towards press freedom, much of the English language media available are little more than outlets for the regime. Those that do have accurate reports are generally exile-movements, not privy to central government information. 30-year-old census data is symptomatic of the weakness of the state over the past few decades and leaves a principal tool for political analysis severely lacking[18]. Newer estimates suggest that the population had doubled to 60 million by 2003[19], whilst updated ethnicity figures are non-existent.

---

[18] The government, in conjunction with the UN have recently announced that they are to carry out a census this year. See: Geoffrey Goddard, "Ministry, UN launch project for first Myanmar census in 30 years," *The Myanmar Times*, http://www.mmtimes.com/index.php/national-news/yangon/3606-ministry-un-launch-project-for-first-myanmar-census-in-30-years.html, (Accessed: 5/1/2013.)
[19] The Ministry of Foreign Affairs Website, "About Myanmar: Population," (2013)

The pace of change in the country has left scholars scrambling to gain theoretical hold on the reform process that has left much of the pre-2008 literature struggling to maintain relevance. With so much now resting on the actions of a small elite it is difficult to predict the political trajectory of the country. Perhaps for these reasons, observers tend to play down decisions and policy formed from within the opaque political hierarchy and focus on the hard facts of the reform process. Oppenheimer points out that these qualities ensure that analysts veer between overemphasising the continuation of the status quo, on the one hand, and predicting widespread change on the other[20]. These factors may go some way in explaining the lack of analysis of the military with regard to the ongoing democratic transition.

2.   Myanmar & Democracy: a conceptual approach

2.1   Democracy and democratic consolidation

Democracy and its components are a highly contested subject and arguably "the most complex concept in political science."[21] This complexity is reflected in the establishment of a multitude of different approaches within the literature. We can divide the theories of the 'raw' concept of democracy into two camps, with proceduralist or minimalist on one side and maximalist or substantial on the other. The procedural minimum concept of democracy, developed by Schumpeter, describes the institutionalisation of political decisions through a "competitive struggle for the peoples vote"[22]. Dahl expanded on this in his concept of polyarchy, developing a broader concept of procedural democracy based on "open contestation [and] public competition"[23], in what is now arguably the most influential concept of democracy within comparative politics. O'Donnell and Schmitter argue that this

---

[20] Michael F Oppenheimer, "From Prediction to Recognition: Using Alternate Scenarios to Improve Foreign Policy Decisions," *SAIS Review* 32, no. 1 (2012): 21.

[21] Carsten Q Schneider and Philippe C Schmitter, "Liberalization, transition and consolidation: measuring the components of democratization," *Democratization* 11, no. 5 (2004): 61.

[22] Joseph A Schumpeter, *Capitalism, Socialism, and Democracy* (London: Harper Perennial Modern Classics, 2008). 242.

[23] R.A. Dahl, *Polyarchy: Participation & Opposition* (New Haven: Yale University Press, 1971). 3.

polycracy creates a stable mix of liberalisation and democratisation that "may have the effect of freezing existing social and economic arrangements"[24].

Other scholars have gone further and developed a concept of liberal democracy, in which institutionally horizontal checks and balances, such as the rule of law and the absence of political interference from the military[25], are analysed to measure this still broader concept of democratisation. Empirical evidence from the 'third-wave' of democratisation would suggest that a large number of newly democratising states do not fulfil many of these criteria, despite greater moves towards liberalisation, indicating "liberalisation and democratization are not synonymous"[26]. They can be classified as 'ambiguous' or 'hybrid' regimes where democratic window-dressing conceals an essentially authoritarian regime[27]. Despite possessing the procedural minimum of democracy, including free and fair elections, the citizens are subject to what O'Donnell et al. call "low intensity citizenship"[28]. Thus, although these states possess political rights enshrined in law, and in some cases checks and balances, the existence of *de facto* informal restrictions "curbs[s] the effective operation of the formal rules and significantly distort[s] their value"[29].

These low-quality democracies have defined the political landscape of SEA for a number of decades, although are there significant differences in the way in which certain democratic institutions have manifested themselves. Croissant and Bünte expand this framework, suggesting that SEA states can be divided into three groups of political regimes[30]. The first group, in which formal democratic institutions co-exist with authoritarian rule or practices,

---

[24] Guillermo O'Donnell, Philippe C Schmitter, and Laurence Whitehead, *Transitions from authoritarian rule: comparative perspectives*, vol. 4 (London: Johns Hopkins University Press, 1986). 12.
[25] Larry Diamond, *Developing Democracy: Toward Consolidation* (Baltimore: Johns Hopkins University Press, 1999). 34.
[26] O'Donnell, Schmitter, and Whitehead, *Transitions from authoritarian rule: comparative perspectives*, 4: 9.
[27] G.A. O'Donnell, *Dissonances: democratic critiques of democracy* (Notre Dame, IN: University of Notre Dame Press, 2007). 54.
[28] O'Donnell, Schmitter, and Whitehead, *Transitions from authoritarian rule: comparative perspectives*, 4: 26.
[29] Aurel Croissant and Marco Bünte, *The Crisis of Democratic Governance in Southeast Asia* (Basingstoke: Palgrave Macmillan, 2011). 3.
[30] Ibid., 3-5.

includes Singapore, Malaysia and Cambodia. Levitsky and Way argue that these states are characterised by the existing regime's use of intimidation, state resources and the media to render the opposition politically impotent [31]. The second group is comprised of "unambiguously authoritarian regimes"[32], with no political or civil space for political pluralism. The third and final are those countries which in the last two decades or so "have experienced a transition to democracy in one way or another"[33], without experiencing any improvement in the democratic quality of the regimes.

Croissant and Bünte's research draws on 2008 data from a selection of democratic indicators supplied by think-tanks, including Freedom House, and no longer reflects the political reality of Myanmar in particular. Freedom House figures from 2013 bear this out, showing an improvement in Myanmar's 'political rights' and 'civil liberties' indicators from those given for 2008[34]. Using Croissant and Bünte's calculus with the revised figures moves Myanmar from the second group to the third group alongside Thailand and the Philippines. Thailand's experience of democratisation, in its cycle of coups and counter coups, typifies the resilience of the nepotistic informal power-structures that underpin third group low-quality democracies. Despite the damning outlook for overall SEA democracy, Crouch argues that Indonesia, comprised of thousands of ethnic groups and a history of armed insurgencies, as well as a legacy of brutal military rule, represents a success of democratisation in the region.[35] Democratic consolidation in the country has gone some way to being fully realised and although challenges and issues remain a broad consensus exists over the success of the Indonesia model.[36]

---

[31] Steven Levitsky and Lucan Way, "The rise of competitive authoritarianism," *Journal of Democracy* 13, no. 2 (2002): 61.
[32] Croissant and Bünte, *The Crisis of Democratic Governance in Southeast Asia*: 5.
[33] Ibid.
[34] Freedom House, "Burma Report," in *Freedom in the World Index* (Freedom House, 2013)
[35] H.A. Crouch, *Political Reform in Indonesia After Soeharto* (Singapore: Institute of Southeast Asian Studies, 2010).
[36] See: E. Aspinall and M. Mietzner, *Problems of Democratisation in Indonesia: Elections, Institutions, and Society* (Singapore: Institute of Southeast Asian Studies, 2010); J. Bertrand, *Nationalism and Ethnic Conflict in Indonesia* (Cambridge: Cambridge University Press, 2004); Aurel Croissant, Paul W. Chambers, and Philip Völkel, "Democracy, the Military and Security Sector Governance in Indonesia,

Alongside the development of the liberal democracy concept during the third-wave era, scholars developed what became known as the 'transitology' paradigm. Rustow identified national unity and conflicts over the rules of the game as the two crucial factors that would initialise the process of democratisation[37]; he thus posited that the democratic transition process involved a pact between the authoritarian and opposition elites, with the leading role taken by the elites. In this paradigm Chan and Shen identify three tasks as essential in successful transition: "to break with the authoritarian past; to seek cooperation with the authoritarian elite; and to come up with a proposal for democratic institution"[38]. This paradigm's strengths lay in its recognition of the elites' role in "[defining] rules and procedures whose configuration will determine likely winners and losers in the future"[39]. Put another way it accounts for the residual impact an ostensibly outgoing regime can have on the future democratic framework and outcome.

Some have argued that, despite the importance of these factors in the implementation of democracy, the paradigm's failure lies in its lack of an account of the nature of authoritarian regimes and their particular social contexts[40]. The transitologist paradigm was severely challenged by hybrid regimes' resistance to democracy during the third-wave of democratisation. Bünte, Chan and Shen argue to overcome this the transitologist approach

---

the Philippines and Thailand," in *The Crisis of Democratic Governance in Southeast Asia*, ed. A. Croissant and M. Bünte (Basingstoke: Palgrave Macmillan, 2011); S.K.M. Tun, *State-Building in Myanmar (1988-2010) and Suharto's Indonesia: A Study of Building a Democratic Developmental State in Myanmar* (Saarbrucken, Germany: Lambert Academic Publishing, 2012).

[37] Dankwart A Rustow, "Transitions to democracy: Toward a dynamic model," *Comparative politics* 2, no. 3 (1970).

[38] Paul Chi-yuen Chan and Simon Shen, "Challenging the Transitoligist Approach: Myanmar's Troubled Democratization," in *Public Governance in Asia and the Limits of Electoral Democracy* ed. B. Bridges and Lock S. Ho (Cheltenham, UK: Edward Elgar Publishing, 2010), 233.

[39] O'Donnell, Schmitter, and Whitehead, *Transitions from authoritarian rule: comparative perspectives*, 4: 6.

[40] Marco Bünte, "Burma's transition to "disciplined democracy": Abdication or institutionalization of military rule?," (GIGA working papers, 2011); Chan and Shen, "Challenging the Transitoligist Approach: Myanmar's Troubled Democratization."; Larry J. Diamond and Doh Chull Shin, *Institutional Reform and Democratic Consolidation in Korea* (Washington, D.C.: Hoover Inst. Press, 1999).

must be augmented with an understanding of the historical and social contexts[41], for "without an empirically detailed and historically grounded understanding of the institutional context, political studies will be filled only with hollow explanations assuming that the elites are simply pursing their own interests"[42]. To understand the reasons why, or why not, the elites choose to democratise in Myanmar, and who these elites actually *are*, a conceptual understanding of historically decisive factors is required.

2.2. Civil-military relations

Military regimes should be distinguished from both other forms of authoritarianism and democracy. Croissant et al. describe civilian control of the military as a prerequisite of a liberal democracy, using Huntingdon's definition of civilian control as: "the extent to which... the armed forces as a whole respond to the direction of the civilian leaders of government."[43] Diamond dubs the presence of a non-elected body that effectively limit the governing power of elected officials as "tutelary authority"[44]. Military bodies that wield these tutelary powers under an ostensibly democratic regime thus create a "tutelary democracy"[45], where important institutional processes are in the hands of the military command. The civil-military relations framework is conceived as a continuum, with full civilian control on one side and military control on the other. With civilian control of the military as a prerequisite, the establishment or re-establishment of civilian control thus becomes a central concern for democratisation.

In congruence with a widening of the security agenda in International Relations literature, recent developments have seen civil-military relations theorists move away from 'coup

---

[41] Bünte, "Burma's transition to "disciplined democracy": Abdication or institutionalization of military rule?."; Chan and Shen, "Challenging the Transitoligist Approach: Myanmar's Troubled Democratization."

[42] Chan and Shen, "Challenging the Transitoligist Approach: Myanmar's Troubled Democratization," 235.

[43] S.P. Huntington, *The Soldier and the State: The Theory and Politics of Civil-Military Relations* (Cambridge: Harvard University Press, 1957). 81.

[44] Diamond, *Developing Democracy: Toward Consolidation*: 7-15.

[45] David Collier and Steven Levitsky, "Democracy with Adjectives: Conceptual Innovation in Comparative Research," *World Politics* 49, no. 03 (1997).

politics' and military rule towards a more general concept of security and security sector governance. This was a result of the perceived inadequacies of theories which merely emphasised the military's direct impact on internal and external security, rather than the newer paradigm of security threats that increasingly transcended international borders[46]. This had led to an increased emphasis on human security, with the use of citizens, rather than the state as the primary referent of security concerns. These theories, while useful in establishing the processes by which effective civilian control over the military can be established, may offer little in the context of SEA states as they suffer from what Collier and Levitsky call "conceptual stretch"[47], rendering it incapable of empirical analysis. A widening of the security agenda thus fails to establish a causal link between civil-military relations and democratic outcomes[48].

Following Lawson, and Croissant et. al, military intervention in politics is conceived as a spectrum[49] of military control of government, military influence and military participation. This, as Bünte and Callahan point out, indicates that the model of civil-military control does not necessarily follow regime type[50]. Democratic regimes can entail some form of military control, just as autocracies can exist under civilian control. The military plays a decisive role in all regimes, either because its existence underpins the very existence of the state or in its decisive role in shaping defence policy and implementation. That the consolidation of democratic regimes requires civilian supremacy in politics points to the suggestion that a move away from authoritarianism will often entail a shift in civil-military relations. To establish what factors underpin these shifts requires a degree of contextualisation.

---

[46]See: David A Baldwin, "The concept of security," *Review of International Studies* 23, no. 1 (1997).
[47] Collier and Levitsky, "Democracy with Adjectives: Conceptual Innovation in Comparative Research," 435.
[48] See: Croissant, Chambers, and Völkel, "Democracy, the Military and Security Sector Governance in Indonesia, the Philippines and Thailand."
[49] Croissant and Bünte, *The Crisis of Democratic Governance in Southeast Asia*; Croissant, Chambers, and Völkel, "Democracy, the Military and Security Sector Governance in Indonesia, the Philippines and Thailand."; Stephanie Lawson, "Conceptual Issues in the Comparative Study of Regime Change and Democratization," *Comparative politics* 25, no. 2 (1993).
[50] Bünte, "Burma's transition to "disciplined democracy": Abdication or institutionalization of military rule?."; Mary Callahan, "The Endurance of Military Rule in Burma: Not Why, But Why Not?'," (2010).

Two theoretical camps have emerged in an attempt to establish this connection[51]. The first relies on an account of internal military variables_while the second highlights external factors in informing degrees of military intervention. As Nordlinger points out however, an absolute separation of these two factors is a false dichotomy[52] as it fails to take into account the interdependence of the two previously ring-fenced concepts. Croissant acknowledges the veracity of this statement but suggests that the division need not entail a lack of understanding[53] of the connections between the two. For the sake of analytical clarity Croissant thus provides an account of mutually interdependent 'push' and 'pull' factors. "Pull" factors as they pull the military into intervention in civil politics and "push" factors as they threaten the internal cohesion and motives of the military and push them away from civil intervention[54]. These factors are thus deemed endogenous and exogenous factors and can be divided into subcategories. Croissant suggests that these subcategories consist of eight variables. The military's personal interests; corporate interests; cohesion; ideology and the configuration of the civilian sphere; economic development; internal security; and external security.[55] Whilst these variables are a useful analytical tool, the literature provides very little consensus as to the content of these subcategories[56], depending instead on context. For the purposes of this paper, these subcategories will be subsumed into two more general umbrella headings.

---

[51] Muthiah Alagappa, *Coercion and Governance: The Declining Political Role of the Military in Asia* (Palo Alto: Stanford University Press, 2001); Callahan, "The Endurance of Military Rule in Burma: Not Why, But Why Not?'."; Larry Jay Diamond, "Thinking about hybrid regimes," *Journal of Democracy* 13, no. 2 (2002).

[52] Eric A Nordlinger, *Soldiers in politics: military coups and governments* (London: Prentice-Hall, 1977). 144.

[53] Aurel Croissant, "Riding the tiger: civilian control and the military in democratizing Korea," *Armed Forces & Society* 30, no. 3 (2004): 359.

[54] Ibid., 360.

[55] Ibid.

[56] See: Mark Beeson and Alex J Bellamy, *Securing Southeast Asia* (London: Routledge, 2007); Bünte, "Burma's transition to "disciplined democracy": Abdication or institutionalization of military rule?."; Croissant and Bünte, *The Crisis of Democratic Governance in Southeast Asia*.

2.21   Endogenous and exogenous factors in military withdrawal

A withdrawal from the political sphere is engendered by the belief among military command that the political conditions are favourable to support the interests of the military overall. Even if there is a desire to withdraw, armies demand sufficient monetary resources to pay staff and equipment costs; if these are not met the stability of the institution itself will come under threat. The independence of the judiciary as an institution may make officers wary of a political withdrawal through the fear of prosecution for atrocities committed prior to this[57]. In some cases, the military may have significant business interests which are only sustainable through continued political participation, especially if the military's activities extend to illegal practices such as drugs or arms dealing. These activities can also impact on the transition towards, and operation of, post-authoritarian regimes as the threat, or implied threat, of the military being able to incite criminal elements in the country may hamper reforms. For these reasons, post-authoritarian governments are often saddled with the legislative or constitutional privileges of the army. Factional and ideological factors can have a significant impact. If an army is divided along ideological, ethnic or class grounds, internal unity is compromised and may impact on its ability to conduct its affairs in the political sphere. Conversely strong cohesion can perpetuate its involvement in politics, especially in the face of factionalised opposition.

Some have argued that military intervention in politics occurs only when the existing or non-military institutional structures are too weak or ineffective to govern the country[58]. Exogenous factors for withdrawal thus stem from the creation or reintroduction of viable institutions with which to usurp military rule. In those countries in which the non-military political culture has been eroded by prolonged periods of military rule, Bünte suggests that

---

[57] Bünte, "Burma's transition to "disciplined democracy": Abdication or institutionalization of military rule?," 11.
[58] Muthiah Alagappa, *Asian Security Practice : Material and Ideational Influences* (Palo Alto: Stanford University Press, 1998), Book; Huntington, *The Soldier and the State: The Theory and Politics of Civil-Military Relations*.

unified and effective civil society movements such as opposition parties, separatist groups or students act as "a vanguard to force the military out of office"[59].

This however may only be a temporary solution if the incoming regime is unable to overcome the lack of institutional structures put in place by the outgoing regime. If the civil society movements aims lack congruence with that of the military, progress towards long term solution may be hampered. These concerns are amplified in situations of successionist or guerilla movements, particularly if any viable political opposition does also not wish to see progress with these conflicts. Military intervention is thus more likely when there is little or no consensus over the political trajectory from any opposition movement and when these movements or groups are themselves fractured. The prevalence of these factors varies from country to country and it is the ways in which endogenous and exogenous factors interact that impact the likelyhood of military withdrawal.

2.22   Historical factors and the establishment of military culture

The endogenous and exogenous factors may explain the continued resilience of military rule but it provides little account of how the dynamic was created in the first place. Singh thus suggests that the contingency of the subcategories on context underpins its unsuitability for use in this instance. The structure is not valid, he argues, as it draws on *a priori* assumptions regarding the structure of western nation states that do not hold in developing and transitional countries and a historical approach should thus be used[60].

Whilst a strict historical approach has its benefits, recent studies on SEA countries have used this broad internal/external framework to successfully analyse civil-military relations and its impact on democratisation[61]. By avoiding a framework which rests on narrow

---

[59] Bünte, "Burma's transition to "disciplined democracy": Abdication or institutionalization of military rule?," 12.
[60] B. Singh, *Civil-military relations in democratising Indonesia: the potentials and limits to change* (Canberra: Strategic and Defence Studies Centre, Australian National University, 2001). 43-5.
[61] See: Diamond and Shin, *Institutional Reform and Democratic Consolidation in Korea*; Crouch, *Political Reform in Indonesia After Soeharto*; Croissant and Bünte, *The Crisis of Democratic*

concepts of western democratic institutions, and instead augmenting an understanding of broad endogenous and exogenous factors with an appreciation of the historical context of both civil and military institutions, a satisfactory balance between empirical and theoretical analysis is reached. Put another way: "what comes first ("even if it was in some sense accidental") conditions what comes later"[62]. This is particularly true in SEA where the institutional structure of the military can often predate those of the state itself. In these situations the residual force of military culture and structure impacts on the later institutions in such a fundamental way that independent analysis of these factors without reference to the 'military impact' becomes impossible.

Whilst a more contemporary continuum of civil-military relations does not assume an apolitical military, it merely assigns the military the role to defend society, not to define it[63]. Croissant notes that the levels of military control in SEA states have been persistent and remained "remarkable stable"[64], despite progress in other areas. In SEA states then the question for this framework is not if the military wields political influence, but how and how much[65]. The political role of the military in SEA should thus be evaluated using a more general framework for military involvement: endogenous and exogenous factors [66]. Disaggregating them in this way allows for a conceptual framework that can be augmented by an appreciation of their interdependence and a contextual awareness.

Governance in Southeast Asia: 190-208; Croissant, "Riding the tiger: civilian control and the military in democratizing Korea."

[62] R.D. Putnam, R. Leonardi, and Rafaella Y. Nanetti, *Making Democracy Work: Civic Traditions in Modern Italy* (Princeton, N.J.: Princeton University Press, 1993). 8.

[63] Richard H Kohn, "How democracies control the military," *Journal of Democracy* 8, no. 4 (1997): 142.

[64] Croissant and Bünte, *The Crisis of Democratic Governance in Southeast Asia*: 194.

[65] Aurel Croissant and David Kuehn, "Civilian Control of the Military and Democracy: Conceptual and Theoretical Perspectives," in *Democracy under Stress: Civil-Military Relations in South and Southeast Asia*, ed. Paul Chambers and Aurel Croissant (Bangkok: ISIS, 2010), 27.

[66] Crouch, *Political Reform in Indonesia After Soeharto*: 288.

3. The Military in Myanmar's politics: from independence to the present day

3.1 The 'reserved domain': establishing the *Tatmadaw* tradition

The Myanmar military (*Tatmadaw*) has a long history of significant involvement in politics and an understanding of the reasons behind contemporary developments is deeply rooted in this fact, "just as it was in 1948, 1958, 1962 and 1988"[67]. Civil war following independence in 1948 was a three-sided affair pitching the Anti-Fascist People's League (AFPFL) under Prime Minister U Nu, the Communist Party and the Karen National Union (KNU) against each other. This followed earlier separate conflicts with ethnic insurgencies on the Bangladesh (then East Bengal) and Chinese borders. The Panglong Agreement of 1947, in which British approved ethnic leaders agreed to become part of the Union of Burma, had given a new political dimension to the ethnic situation that existed in the country.

With this backdrop, the AFPFL was originally formed in a merger between Aung Sang's Burma National Army (BNA), the Communist Party (CPB) and the People's Revolutionary Party led by U Nu, first with the assistance of the Japanese to fight British colonialism and later to resist Japanese colonial ambitions. These political origins ensured that the army saw itself as a "political force first and a military force second"[68], the officer corps in particular drew heavily on ideology that emphasised their role as freedom fighters, not professional soldiers. In the absence of a unifying threat following the departure of the Japanese and eventually the British, ethnic and ideological divisions within the army became more pronounced, and the CPB and a large faction of the BNA disbanded from the AFPFL to join the rebellion, either fighting for the KNU or the communists. During this period a core of approximately 10,000 troops remained loyal to the government and supported it though the civil war while simultaneously combating CIA-backed Kuomintang and Chinese-backed communist insurgencies.

---

[67] Robert Taylor, "Myanmar: military politics and the prospects for democratisation," *Asian Affairs* 29, no. 1 (1998): 5.
[68] Ibid., 7.

By 1958 the AFPFL government was forced to split and the army stepped in to act as caretaker under General Ne Win for a period of two years. The British colonial policy of privileging the Christian Karen group over the majority Bamars in military and administrative matters had ensured that the relatively diverse military body prior to independence now resembled a Bamar army, as other ethnic groups disbanded to fight for their 'own' causes throughout the civil war, alienated by a Bamar backlash against this perceived injustice [69]. Those Karen officers that had remained following this were suspended. This had the duel effect of "freeing the *Tatmadaw* of [internal] ethnic- and ideology- based conflicts"[70] and further sharpening the Bamar/ethnic distinction in the ongoing conflicts.

The civil war had also forced the institutional modernisation of the military which could not be matched by the civilian institutions, prompting the *Tatmadaw* to expand its political influence in the fulfilment of these roles. During the caretaker government era the now primarily Bamar *Tatmadaw* thus developed a "praetorian ethos"[71] as the sole defender and unifier of the country to such an extent that by 1958 the *Tatmadaw* claimed between 30 and 40 percent of the national budget[72]. Elections were held in 1960 and U Nu subsequently re-elected,

Following U Nu's re-election in 1960 the government thus set about trying to find the solution to long-term peace that had eluded the country since independence, through the creation of two more ethnic states, Mon and Arakan (now Rakhine state). As with the creation of the original five ethnic states in 1947, these did little to actually appease the calls for autonomy as they were still fiscally and militarily linked to the central state. Taylor suggests that the state's obfuscation of ethnic issues and subsequent failure to address the

---

[69] Taylor, *The State in Myanmar*: 234.
[70] Kyaw Yin Hlaing, "Setting the rules for survival: why the Burmese military regime survives in an age of democratization," *The Pacific Review* 22, no. 3 (2009): 275.
[71] Bünte, "Burma's transition to "disciplined democracy": Abdication or institutionalization of military rule?," 32.
[72] Taylor, *The State in Myanmar*: 338.

root cause of the problem was deeply rooted in the view that there was "no logical limit to nationalist claims"[73], a paranoia that continues to exist today. These ethnic concerns characterised a key difference between the political outlook of the *Tatmadaw* and the civilian government of U Nu, sowing the seeds for later justifications for military control as a preventative measure to prevent the emergence of any autonomous centres of influence and the subsequent 'disintegration of the union'.

When in 1961 a coup plot was uncovered among key members of the *Tatmadaw*, U Nu's government requested that Ne Win remove the offending officers. Far from neutralising the political ambitions of the *Tatmadaw* this laid the foundations for the successful coup staged the following year. By allowing Ne Win to remove voices of dissent from among the *Tatmadaw* it concentrated power solely in the upper echelons of military command, with him at the apex. On the 2nd March 1962 the newly formed Revolutionary Council, under Ne Win, seized power and established a Leninist military backed political party known as the Burma Socialist Program Party (BSPP). It immediately abolished the 1947 constitution (and with it the "destabilising effects of the autonomous areas"[74]), nationalised the economy under the direction of the 'Burmese Way to Socialism' and cut all ties with the outside world.

Although student demonstrations in 1974 prompted the ceremonial return of constitutional power and the staging of 'state-led' elections, the core functions of the state remained in *Tatmadaw* hands, with the majority of cabinet and other crucial offices solely occupied by military officers[75]. Ne Win occupied all important offices of state throughout this time and effective power was channelled through him. Kyaw Yin Hlaing draws comparisons between Ne Win and Mao Zedong in his exercise of "power to appoint and dismiss...state and party

---

[73] Ibid., 289.
[74] D. Brown, *The State and Ethnic Politics in South-East Asia* (London: Routledge, 1994). 19.
[75] Taylor, *The State in Myanmar*: 318-21.

officials at all levels"[76]. He consolidated his power during the socialist period through regular purges and through the creation of deliberate disunity among his subordinates, ensuring that their loyalties lay only with him.

These summary dismissals and appointments had an impact on implementation of policy at all levels of government. As accountability was directed only towards Ne Win, subordinates at the regional level performed their duties "with the single aim of seeking the chairman's approval"[77]. The uncertainty that characterised his leadership also ensured that regional and divisional levels of government retreated singularly into their own spheres of influence in an attempt to avoid confrontation with other officials and thus the scrutiny of Ne Win. Over time would serve to form "part of the institutional culture of the *Tatmadaw*"[78].

By the mid 1980s the socialist autarky of the preceding 25 years had begun to take its toll. The nationalised businesses of the 1960s had failed to generate the economic surpluses the state had hoped to rely upon and the repayment of international loans, grudgingly accepted in the 1970s, was due. By 1987 the UN had labelled the country with Least Developed Country status, confirming in the minds of the Burmese people the failure of the previous 26 years[79]. The regime's preoccupation with the ethnic concerns in the face of an impending economic crisis was revealed when it moved to close down the cross border trading areas that generated income for the KNU and other groups derived most of their income. This closed off the black market supply of consumer goods from Thailand, depriving many ordinary citizens of their primary source of income and further fuelling inflation[80]. A neglected and underdeveloped financial system was thus left with little choice but to demonetise the currency, wiping out 25 percent of the value of the money supply overnight

---

[76] Hlaing, "Setting the rules for survival: why the Burmese military regime survives in an age of democratization," 276.
[77] Ibid.
[78] Ibid., 277.
[79] K.S. Koh, *Misunderstood Myanmar: An Introspective Study of a Southeast Asian State in Transition* (Singapore: Humanities Press, 2011). 122.
[80] Taylor, *The State in Myanmar*: 377.

on 3rd November 1985[81]. Twelve months of stagnation and political deadlock followed, culminating in further a further demonetisation initiative.

Demonstrations that had begun in Yangon in September 1987 by students unable to pay their tuition fees had by June 1988 spread to other parts of the city and country. The administrative functions of the government were paralysed by the economic conditions and political inaction engendered by political deference as administrators waited for "Ne Win to tell them what to do"[82]. The announcement that Ne Win would step down on 23rd July left the remaining military/BSPP framework rudderless and ensured the continued escalation of unrest. Civil servants and supporters of the regime began to join the ranks of the protesters as wages went unpaid and the emerging opposition groups were left factionalised and unable to present a united front in the face of the rising discontent. By August the *Tatmadaw* was the only remaining operationally viable institution in the country and was faced with the prospect of a complete depletion of all its supply reserves as protesters across the country shut down oil refineries and transport routes. Faced with this ultimatum and the threat of ethnic insurgencies exploiting the unrest to make major advances in the border areas[83], the *Tatmadaw* felt they were forced to act.

In what became known as the 8888 movement the protesters were galvanised and began a more organised system of strikes, culminating in the general strike of 8th August 1988. The army moved in as the number of protesters swelled and widespread looting began. As the tide began to turn and the students and activists began to perceive the army's victory as inevitable they fled in their thousands to insurgent camps along the Thai border. The estimates of the number killed in the months following as the army attempted to consolidate its control over the country range from 10,000 to 1000[84], with many thousands more arrested. By the 18th September the *Tatmadaw* had established control and set about

---

[81] This figure is disputed. Koh puts the figure at between 60 and 80 percent. See: Koh, *Misunderstood Myanmar: An Introspective Study of a Southeast Asian State in Transition*: 121.
[82] Taylor, *The State in Myanmar*: 385.
[83] Ibid., 386.
[84] Ibid., 388.

establishing the State Law and Order Restoration Council (SLORC), under direct military rule. To the *Tatmadaw* it seemed that, once again, the army alone were able to ensure the survival of the country.

The *Tatmadaw* set about revoking the 1974 constitution and the immediate dissolving of parliament, establishing total military dominance across the executive, legislative and judicial domains. Despite his apparent withdrawal from power, Ne Win continued to exert significant influence over the military with senior officials still seeking his blessing for Council decisions[85]. Institutionally the perception was of being above politics; indeed when interviewed on the subject of the '88 uprising some members of the *Tatmadaw* asserted that the "protesters didn't even know what they were protesting for"[86]. This was symptomatic of the paternalist nature of the *Tatmadaw* in their belief that they singularly capable of determining the political trajectory in Myanmar.

Despite the monolithic structure of the *Tatmadaw* in this period, the leadership of Saw Muang was not hegemonic like that of Ne Win. Although the regime was united enough to resist any opposition[87], it continued to operate in largely autonomous spheres throughout the country, with regional commanders operating almost independently of Yangon. This in turn bred widespread corruption that entrenched the *Tatmadaw* further. Like their counterparts in Indonesia and Thailand, the military began to develop significant business interests, eventually becoming the most significant business actor in the country[88]. This had the effect of extending informal patronage networks down from the *Tatmadaw* command towards peripheral business elites and further entrenching the military rule. Despite formally

---

[85] Hlaing, "Setting the rules for survival: why the Burmese military regime survives in an age of democratization," 278.
[86] Koh, *Misunderstood Myanmar: An Introspective Study of a Southeast Asian State in Transition*: 125.
[87] Kyaw Yin Hlaing, "Power and factional struggles in post-independence Burmese governments," *Journal of Southeast Asian Studies* 39, no. 01 (2008): 163.
[88] A. Selth, *Burma's armed forces: power without glory* (Norwalk, Conn.: EastBridge, 2002). 130.

adopting a market led economy in the 1990s, the economy remained almost exclusively in the hands of the military[89].

Conflating business interests and those of the government ensures that the military will pursue policies which perpetuate these interests. In many ways this system of power adopted by the *Tatmadaw* reflected the pre-colonial hierarchy of the *mandala* system in which largely autonomous outlying areas paid tribute to the greater centres of power[90]. Whilst this ensured that the apex of the hierarchy controlled the broad trajectory of policy, it left regional commanders free to pursue more short-term goals as long as it did not interfere with central policy. Practically this meant that regional commanders were more interested in the military defeat of the ethnic insurgents in their respective areas than any peace agreements pursued by Yangon; a policy that continues to this day[91].

Following the traditions of the caretaker government of the 1960s the regime of Saw Muang had promised the handover of military power following elections of 1990. The military government refused to acknowledge the landslide victory of the NLD in May 1990, arguing that the country lacked the constitutional basis for such a power transfer. ASSK was placed under house arrest and the opposition silenced, leading to the widespread international criticism that was to continue for decades. The military thus began a new process of erecting long-term safeguards to its political power, while continuing to outwardly state its desire to move towards democratisation.

To support the new emphasis on development and reconciliation SLORC was renamed the State Peace and Development Council (SPDC) in 1997. In addition to the *Tatmadaw's* policy of expanding its business interests, it set about increasing the size of the army significantly. Throughout the early 1980s the ethnic insurgent groups had often been better

---

[89] Heritage Foundation, "Burma," *2013 Index of Economic Freedom*,
http://www.heritage.org/index/country/burma, (Accessed: 27/02/2013.)
[90] Terwiel, *Thailand's Political History: From the 13th Century to Recent Times*: 22.
[91] Aung Hla Tun, "Myanmar rebels say army ignoring president's ceasefire," *Reuters*, 20/02/2013,
http://www.reuters.com/article/2013/01/20/us-myanmar-kachin-idUSBRE90J03820130120,
(Accessed: 03/02/2013.)

equipped and more than able to match the *Tatmadaw*. From 1988 to 2004 the size of the standing army increased from 186,000 to 370,000[92]. This helped to support the negotiation position in agreeing the ceasefires with the ethnic insurgency groups put in place in late 1990s. By militarising the *Tatmadaw* aims were self fulfilling as ethnic groups increased its capabilities in response. The funding of this saw such groups come into direct conflict with the *Tatmadaw's* narcotics trade and increased conflict in the border regions[93].

The increased militarisation also provided logistical backup for the infrastructure programs that the Junta hoped would expand economic output. The *Tatmadaw* managed to largely circumvent the international sanctions placed on Myanmar in the 2000s through the sale of natural gas and hydroelectric power to India, China and Thailand, reducing its exposure to external pressure[94]. The business interests of the *Tatmadaw* helped to safeguard its interests in two ways: firstly, some of the revenues allowed direct support for the increase in military wages and running costs and secondly it allowed the creation of the army as a privileged social-elite. Military officers are entitled to free or subsidised healthcare, education and housing as well as travel and other privileges denied the average citizen. This was a tradition started in the Ne Win era with the construction of a military housing complex for retired and serving officers in Yangon[95]. In addition to exacerbating the social divisions between the army and regular citizens, it also further underscored the ethnic divisions between the Bamar heartland and the ethic periphery as 80% of the *Tatmadaw* are ethnically Bamar[96].

[92] Mary Callahan, *Making Enemies: War and State Building in Burma* (Ithaca, N.Y.: Cornell University Press, 2003); Selth, *Burma's armed forces: power without glory*.
[93] Christina Fink, "Militarization in Burma's ethnic states: causes and consequences," *Contemporary Politics* 14, no. 4 (2008): 453.
[94] Kyaw Yin Hlaing, "Understanding Recent Political Changes in Myanmar," *Contemporary Southeast Asia: A Journal of International and Strategic Affairs* 34, no. 2 (2012).
[95] Hlaing, "Setting the rules for survival: why the Burmese military regime survives in an age of democratization," 283.
[96] Alfred Stepan, Juan J Linz, and Yogendra Yadav, *Crafting State-Nations: India and other multinational democracies* (Baltimore: Johns Hopkins University Press, 2011). 267.

3.2 From direct rule to "disciplined democracy": the guiding hand of the *Tatmadaw* in contemporary Myanmar

The *Tatmadaw* thus began the current process of a return to nominally civilian rule once it had established a political framework in which its core cultural and political interests were protected. This amounts to a change in the dynamic between endogenous and exogenous factors. Specifically, the *Tatmadaw* embarked on a modernisation program which conflated its interests with that of the state. The withdrawal from military control was thus fully realised through the mitigating of endogenous factors, beginning with the reforms in early 2000s up to the present day. The political changes that have been instigated, however, do not amount a full withdrawal from politics and the irreversible transition to democracy that some have asserted, as the military still maintains effective control over all levels of the political process. Its perception of ethnic secessionism and the associated fear of the disintegration of the Union have led to erecting further safeguards to its power. By co-opting the NLD into the political process it has factionalised the opposition, both internally within the NLD and between the NLD and the ethnic groups.

The current process was begun in 2003 by General Khin Nyunt, following his appointment as Prime Minister of the SPDC. The announcement of the 'roadmap' to disciplined democracy put forward on this occasion aimed to establish a civilian government and a new constitution. This 'roadmap' consisted of seven steps: (1) Reconvening of the National Convention; (2) the implementation of the process necessary for a genuine and disciplined democratic system; (3) Drafting of a new constitution; (4) Adoption of the constitution through national referendum; (5) Holding of free and fair elections; (6) Convening of parliament; (7) establishment of a modern, developed and democratic nation[97]. The NLD agreed to the reconvening of the National Convention on the condition that ASSK was released, and the party offices allowed to re-open; the SPDC refused. The political impasse did not come to a head again until the crackdown on the Saffron Uprising of 2007, sparked

---

[97] "Mass rally supports seven-point roadmap clarified by Prime Minister," *The New Light of Myanmar*, 20/09/2003, http://www.ibiblio.org/obl/docs/rallies-etc..htm, (Accessed: 07/01/2013.)

by the *Sangha's* protests at rising fuel prices. International pressure reached an all-time high following widespread press coverage of the uprising, and there was hope that military rule was under threat.

Under intense UN and ASEAN pressure the drafting of a new constitution was finalised in February 2008 and in May 2008 was formally adopted following a referendum. The results of 98 percent voter turnout and 94.4 percent in favour prompted widespread accusations of manipulation[98]. The adoption of the new constitution represents *de jure* protection of *Tatmadaw* interests in its stipulation that the one quarter of all *Pyihtaungsu Hluttaw* (National Legislative Assembly) should be reserved for *Tatmadaw* personnel. By placing the Ministry of Home affairs under direct military control and barring candidates with non-Burmese spouses from taking presidential office[99], the constitution further undermines hopes for meaningful opposition engagement.

For the elections of November 2010 the military created its own proxy party, the United Solidarity and Development Party (USDP). Former military commanders resigned from the army and joined its ranks, led by current president Thein Sein, fully bankrolled by the military. The electoral system was tilted heavily in favour of the USDP from the very beginning, with the opposition facing high registration fees and the NLD spilt over ASSK's decision to boycott the election. A splinter group, the National Democratic Front, was formed from NLD defectors and went on to win a handful of seats in the *Hluttaw* legislature. The USDP won an overall majority with 80 percent in the lower house and 77 percent in the upper house, again overshadowed by accusations of vote manipulation[100]. Despite this, the outward face of reform since the election has taken many by surprise in its speed and scope. July 2011 saw the NLD welcomed back into the political arena and in the

---

[98] "Myanmar formally announces ratification of new constitution draft," *People's Daily Online*, 30/05/2008, http://english.people.com.cn/90001/90777/90851/6421254.html, (Accessed: 14/01/2013.)
[99] Aung Sang Suu Kyi was married to a Briton, Michael Evis, until his death in 1999
[100] ICG (International Crisis Group), "Myanmar's Post-Election Landscape," *Crisis Group Asia Briefing*, no. 118, March (2011).

by-elections of 2012 they secured 43 seats in *Amyotha Hluttaw*[101]. Media censorship has largely been abandoned, and state run newspapers no longer carry long established propaganda statements. Civil society activism was bolstered by the cancellation of the Myitsone dam project and opposition groups legitimised in the NLD members shift from activists to active parliamentarians. Following these developments EU and US sanctions have been lifted and Naypyitaw has welcomed several high profile visits from foreign dignitaries including Barack Obama and David Cameron[102]. This legitimisation in the eyes of the international community has allowed the *Tatmadaw* the domestic political space with which to carry out the reforms that cement its position in power.

The military transition since 2011 has also seen a huge wave of privatisations, with over 270 state-owned companies sold to former military commanders or their cronies[103]. Foreign investment has expanded massively; conspicuously absent firms such as Coca-Cola now maintain a presence in the country[104] and international banks and consultancies have full time staff in Yangon for the first time. International ATMs have recently come online, vastly expanding the business and tourism capacity. Despite weakening direct military power, the sale consolidates informal power among Thein Sein and other military leaders. This has further bolstered the business elites within the country and the networks of patronage that exist between them and the military[105].

---

[101] ICG (International Crisis Group), "Reform in Myanmar: One Year On," *Crisis Group Asia Briefing*, no. 136, April (2012).

[102] Julie Pace, "Obama makes history with Myanmar, Cambodia visits," *Associated Press*, 20/11/2012, http://bigstory.ap.org/article/obama-myanmar-show-power-new-beginning, (Accessed: 07/02/2013.)

[103] "Govt property auction nets K800b," *The Myanmar Times*, http://www.mmtimes.com/index.php/national-news/yangon/3606-ministry-un-launch-project-for-first-myanmar-census-in-30-years.html, (Accessed: 5/1/2013.)

[104] Martinne Geller, "Coke ships first drinks to Myanmar in decades," *Reuters*, 10/09/2012, http://www.reuters.com/article/2012/09/10/us-cocacola-myanmar-idUSBRE8890MW20120910, (Accessed: 15/12/2012.)

[105] Patrick Barta, "Final Frontier: Firms Flock to Newly Opened Myanmar," *The Wall Street Journal*, http://online.wsj.com/article/SB10000872396390443749204578050773460553586.html, (Accessed: 02/02/2013.)

Despite significant progress, the transition still represents little more than a constitutionalistion of de facto military rule. As well as direct control of the Ministry of Home Affairs, the most recent cabinet reshuffle in September 2012 appointed 26 of the 30 cabinet positions to *Tatmadaw* personnel [106]. The 25 percent military quota in the *Pyihtaungsu Hluttaw* and the veto power this instils ensures that any change will be at the behest of the military itself. By establishing the National Defence and Security Council (NDSC), now the most powerful institution in the country[107], the *Tatmadaw* effectively controls all aspects of defence policy and implementation, internally and externally. Unlike Thailand in which the King acts as a counter balance to the power of the military, the *Tatmadaw* effective operates alone in the political sphere. One can conclude that the constitution has enshrined in law a "competitive military regime, in which... [the *Tatmadaw*] remains the arbiter of power"[108].

The patronage networks that intimately connect former military men with political and business actors represent a guarantee of military interests in the political sphere. The growing economy and increasing international engagement lay the theoretical framework that underpins the potential establishment of effective democratic institutions. If this can be utilised it can carry the political process forwards, and with it the interests of the current generation of military leaders. By establishing a political space for former military men in the new constitutional arrangement, the army has overcome threats of internal factionalism and the possibility of succession conflicts. The opening up a political space to the NLD and other opposition has created a political 'pressure valve' that neutralised the ability to mount an effective challenge to military control. This, in conjunction with the international recognition the regime now receives, has served to bolster its domestic legitimacy. This paper has shown how despite a largely favourable change in endogenous factors the army

---

[106] Aung Hla Tun, "Myanmar president promotes reformers in cabinet shake-up," *Reuters*, 27/08/2012, http://www.reuters.com/article/2012/08/27/us-myanmar-politics-idUSBRE87Q0QG20120827, (Accessed: 08/02/2013.)
[107] Hlaing, "Understanding Recent Political Changes in Myanmar," 202.
[108] Bünte, "Burma's transition to "disciplined democracy": Abdication or institutionalization of military rule?," 18.

does not seem prepared to begin a total withdrawal from the political arena. The army's reluctance to commit to a formal withdrawal is thus a result of exogenous factors, namely the existence and perceived threat of the ethnic groups.

The reasons behind this stem from a fear of ethnic insurgents and their leaders, borne, as I have shown, out of a historical obsession with the unity of the country. By taking sole control of the NDSC the *Tatmadaw* has signalled the seriousness with which it takes this. Koh stresses the importance of the historical dimension of the ethnic question on why the *Tatmadaw* is unwilling to tackle the ethnic issue head on. When questioned on why the ethnic issue was such a crucial stumbling block, a senior former general stated: "We fear the repeat of history.... history has object lessons...which truly will not "wither away""[109]. This mutual mistrust on the part of the ethnic leaders and the *Tatmadaw*, however, is not just a result of the cultural factors and internal structure of the military outlined above, but also in the recent actions of the ethnic leaders and the NLD. By committing itself to a flawed political process that sees the ethnic groups marginalised, the NLD has alienated itself from any possibility of unification with them. In a political system that the *Tatmadaw* have designed to cement their power base the opportunities for a resolution of the ethnic question within the system seem slim. The formation of the ethnic groups and the internal dynamic both between factions and between the broader opposition base is vital to an understanding of this. An appreciation of the tri-partite nature of the dynamic between the *Tatmadaw, the* ethnic groups and the possibility of an opposition alliance thus underlies Myanmar's final obstacle towards the consolidation of democracy.

4. Mutual mistrust: the *Tatmadaw*, ethnicity, ethnonationalism, and ethnic conflict

In early and pre-modern societies cultural systems were based on religious and dynastic connections. The modern construct is thus based on what Anderson has famously dubbed

---

[109] Koh, *Misunderstood Myanmar: An Introspective Study of a Southeast Asian State in Transition*: 142.

"imagined communities"[110]. The emergence of the nation state and national identity that were superimposed on these existing communities thus created tensions during subsequent attempts at nation building. Colonialism, as with other countries in the region, signalled the starting point for the ethnic tensions that exist in Myanmar today.

As a province of the British Raj, Myanmar was subject to a one-size-fits-all colonial policy that was implemented across the sub-continent from the seat of colonial power in New Delhi. The resultant British policy made no attempt at nation building; Myanmar was to act as a buffer for the protection of the Raj first, and as source of raw materials second. Divide-and-rule policy was implemented with little thought as to the ethnic or cultural realities of the country and was unevenly implemented. The effect of this was to reshape the hierarchies of rule in the country, particularly in the ethnic Bamar heartland, while leaving the periphery largely unaffected. In this way the British reshaped the previous perceptions of ethnicity in Myanmar while privileging the ethnic minorities of the periphery over the Bamar majority[111].

The colonial army in particular was comprised mostly of ethnic minorities, with the Christian Karen occupying the upper echelons of the indigenous officer corps. Different ethnic groups fought for both the Allies and the Japanese during WWII so that by the time of independence the ethnic divisions were further underscored by new ideological and cultural differences. The 1947 Panglong Agreement, still used as a referent today, was based largely on the now accepted colonial perceptions of ethnicity. This colonial legacy was to form the basis of further constitutions, to the extent that 1974 constitution still used the colonial descriptors of ethnicity to establish the seven Bamar divisions and seven ethnic states now enshrined in the 2008 constitution.

---

[110] Benedict Anderson, *Imagined communities: Reflections on the origin and spread of nationalism* (London: Verso, 1991).
[111] Thant Myint-U, *The River of Lost Footsteps: Histories of Burma* (London: Faber and Faber, 2007).

The constitutional process of the past 20 years has been the overriding platform for the articulation of ethnic claims outside the military sphere, and in many ways is the greatest obstacle it faces, despite the greater emphasis on the NLD and opposition politics. The reluctance to tackle the issue head on has meant the 2008 constitution offered no concessions to the ethnic question. Chapters one and two merely reiterate the basic structure of the ethnic divisions, originally stipulated in the Panglong Agreement, and the process for redrawing state boundaries, subject in practice to a military veto[112]. The stipulation in chapter seven that all areas of defence policy are under Tatmadaw control is the most significant for any attempts at an ethnic peace process. This, in effect, frames the deadlock that underlies the impossibility of any attempts at reconciliation.

The political reality, outside of the constitutional process, has seen a concerted effort since independence towards the creation of a national identity based on Bamar Buddhist values. The various guises of the *Tatmadaw* as the "perpetual junta"[113] have to varying degrees attempted to foster a rally-round-the-flag nationalism based on the Bamar language, religion and identity. This has alienated, and in many cases antagonised the ethnic minorities and through its ethnocentricity has effectively restricted the scope of a solution to military means alone.

Indeed, the military based regimes have found their reflection in the militaries of the various ethnic groups. By uniquely framing the situation as a military one, the ethnic groups are forced to respond in kind. This forces the military to provide some respite from the at times brutal conflict with various ceasefires[114]. The merry-go-round of ceasefires and resumptions of hostility only serve to perpetuate the problem through an entrenchment of military culture on both sides. This is also in part due to hardliners in both the *Tatmadaw* and the ethnic groups still framing the issue in a way that has little bearing on reality. The simultaneous

---

[112] Government of Myanmar, "Constitution of the Republic of the Union of Myanmar," (Naypyitaw: Ministry of Information, 2008)
[113] Callahan, "The Endurance of Military Rule in Burma: Not Why, But Why Not?'."
[114] Ian Holliday, "Ethnicity and Democratization in Myanmar," *Asian Journal of Political Science* 18, no. 2 (2010): 117.

acknowledgment of the existence of the ethnic groups (albeit a thin one) and the maintenance of ethnic armies and their autonomy on the one side, and the infallibility of the unification of the country on the other amounts to little more than a political fudge. This is not to suggest that the *Tatmadaw* have been weak in their handling of the issue, nor that the ethnic groups have no right to their claims, but it does demonstrate unwillingness to consider non-military solutions.

Opposition groups, such as the NLD, despite their public face, have in reality played an equal part in the failure, through their reluctance to face up to the ethnic question. Once the military was confident of the protection of its interests it exploited this failure on the part of the NLD. Seeing an opening into the democratic process the NLD ultimately felt that by becoming part of the system, the ethnic question would resolve itself. In fact, the military's transition to disciplined democracy was a calculation based on a fear of NLD and ethnic alliance. By becoming democratic the *Tatmadaw* was able to entice the NLD into the political fold and in doing so it forced the NLD to cede political objectives. The subsequent perception among the ethnic groups was that the NLD had acquiesced to military dominance and thus forfeited any claim to represent the political ambitions of the ethnic groups. This claim has become more pronounced since the re-election of ASSK as NLD leader in March 2013.[115]

Figure 1 suggests that the ethnic areas are areas which can be clearly ring fenced and categorised. Whilst a useful illustration, in reality both the geographical location and the ways in which the people actually categorise themselves are impossible to determine in a country with so little social scientific research[116]. This trait also highlights the impossibility of categorising the political commitments of the different groups. The opposition and the

---

[115] Kyaw Thu, "Suu Kyi Seeks Closer Army Ties After Re-Election as Party Leader," *Businessweek*, 10/03/2013, http://www.businessweek.com/news/2013-03-10/myanmar-s-opposition-party-elects-aung-san-suu-kyi-as-chairwoman, (Accessed: 10/03/2013.); "Aung San Suu Kyi tells of fondness for Burma army," *BBC News*, 27/01/2013, http://www.bbc.co.uk/news/uk-21217884, (Accessed: 10/02/2013.)
[116] Ian Holliday, *Burma Redux: Global Justice and the Quest for Political Reform in Myanmar* (New York: Columbia University Press, 2012). 131.

ethnic groups are divided today precisely because of the wide divergence in many of their political aims. In its limited policy manifestos the NLD pays lip service to an idea of multiculturalism, based on what Walton calls the "myth of Panglong"[117]. He asserts that the NLD believe that multiculturalism is already a reality in Myanmar and only a democratic process is restricting it. Smith thus argues that democracy is the primary issue for the NLD and the ethic question merely second[118]. By subscribing to the colonial terminology and classifications of ethnicity the NLD obfuscates the ethnic question and misinterprets the causal link between them. A multicultural model is unachievable until a democratic system that that includes the full participation of the ethnic groups is put in place. Until the issue is redefined in an appropriate way, democracy cannot be fully realised.

5. Summary. 'Jobs for the boys': how ethnic conflict perpetuates the military's role in politics

Some have touted federalism as a method of overcoming the ethnic question in a transition towards liberal democracy[119], arguing that ethnic identity is now so entrenched as to render all other solutions impossible. Marcus Brand argues at length that the 2008 constitution is in fact a "quasi-federal" model, and indeed that its previous constitutions have had federal elements since as early as the Panglong Agreement[120]. That the military continues to operate effectively outside of a constitutional framework through its veto renders this fact inconsequential. The *Tatmadaw's* operating outside of the constitution is a result of its deep seated fear of a breakup of the union and the reason why it continues to frantically reiterate its overarching aim of non disintegration from the union. It is also important to note that while ethnic state and federal systems can operate concurrently, they are not one and the

---

[117] Matthew J Walton, "Ethnicity, conflict, and history in Burma: The myths of Panglong," *Asian Survey* 48, no. 6 (2008).
[118] Alan Smith, "Ethnicity and federal prospect in Myanmar," in *Federalism in Asia*, ed. B. He, B. Galligan, and T. Inoguchi (Cheltenham: Edward Elgar, 2009), 191.
[119] Ibid.
[120] Marcus Brand, "'A bird in the hand...' The federal pattern of Myanmar's 2008 Constitution," (Unpublished work. Used with author's permission, 2012)

same. As discussed previously, the problem of demarcation of these and the elastic nature of the self-perception of identity highlights the problem with the conflation of two.

The emphasis on stability as the primary referent of Myanmar's security is framed primarily in terms of the ethnic threat, and to a lesser extent malign external forces. In attempts to justify the continued justification of the military Thein Sein takes advantage of an improved international legitimacy to frame the ethnic question strictly as a threat to the democratic process. In an interview he stated: "If we put racial and religious issues at the forefront.... the country's stability peace and the democratization process could be severely affected and much would be lost"[121]. By framing it in this way the *Tatmadaw* justify the continued existence of the militarisation of the state. Borne out of this fear is the military's refusal to entirely disengage from politics and creates a situation whereby the development of non-military institutions of governance and effective hierarchies of power are not allowed to develop to a point where they are self-sufficient.

When discussing the colonial legacy, Koh notes that this lack of effective institutions in Myanmar post-independence, and indeed up until the present day, was down to British colonial government's failure to allow the "Myanmas [Burmese] any discretion either in policy formulation or policy implementation.[122]" The *Tatmadaw's* political legacy can thus been seen as an extension of British colonial policy. By positioning itself as 'above politics' and as the sole saviour of the state, preventing a slide into anarchy, the *Tatmadaw* itself emulates the neglect of British colonial regime. By militarising the state it has failed to develop an independent institutional framework which is capable of the effective construction and implementation of policy. Although economic growth and plural participation may help to offset this in the long-run, the exclusion of the ethnic question entirely would allow only for the development of an ethnocentric Bamar framework.

---

[121] BBC HARDtalk, "BBC HARDtalk Interview - U Thein Sein - President of Burma [VIDEO]," 8/1/2013, http://www.youtube.com/watch?v=7dP6ohVYYAg, (Accessed: 1/02/2013.)
[122] Koh, *Misunderstood Myanmar: An Introspective Study of a Southeast Asian State in Transition*: 105.

The *Tatmadaw* culture, borne out of its historical development that emphasises top down hierarchy, has meant that decisions are made on an arbitrary basis, often without a consensus view. This is true today, both in the military veto and the lack of any true opposition engagement by the USDP. This political culture is useful in ensuring implementation of policy but not in fostering a more long term strategy to establish political trajectory. Thus while the military institutions that served the functions of the state are capable to some degree, the political myopia that the *Tatmadaw* suffers is to some extent responsible for its failure to bolster the development of institutions outside the military framework. As Watts notes, there is an important distinction between "constitutional form and operational reality"[123] in any analysis of the constitutional framework. In Myanmar the principle challenge in ensuring the constitution is as good as its promises is thus creating effective institutions independently from military interference.

6.   Conclusion: looking to the future

The very existence of the ethnic insurgent groups, and the recent upsurge in the incidents of conflict, has been directly cited by the military in support of its continued direct political engagement[124]. The opposition too is little interested in finding any long term solution to the ethnic problems, preferring instead, to focus on the process of securing its place in the political system and overcoming internal divisions[125]. It seems likely that in the face of a 'common enemy' the alliance between opposition groups and a broad base of ethnic groups will survive until at least the 2015 elections. At some point, however, the NLD may be forced to concede further some aspect of the peace process in order to achieve some of the democratic aims. It is not an either/or process, but given the current political trajectory, a

---

[123] Ronald L Watts, *Comparing federal systems in the 1990s* (Kingston, Ont.: Institute of Intergovernmental Relations, Queen's University, 1996). 75.
[124] Aye Aye Win, "Myanmar general defends military's political role," *Associated Press*, 27/3/2012, http://www.guardian.co.uk/world/feedarticle/10165291, (Accessed: 8/01/2013.)
[125] Thomas Fuller, "In Public Eye, Shining Star of Myanmar Loses Luster," *The New York Times*, 09/03/2013, http://www.nytimes.com/2013/03/10/world/asia/in-public-eye-shining-star-of-myanmar-loses-luster.html, (Accessed: 9/03/2013.)

'two-speed' Myanmar seems a possibility and the leaders of the ethnic groups may begin to perceive the democratic reforms to be further entrenching the interests of Bamar majority only.

Unless the NLD has the political foresight to realise both that the ethnic question is the primary issue and that without an alliance with the ethnic groups it will remain unable to challenge military control of the political system. As the economy expands, and FDI flows in the coming years there is a risk that unchecked growth will create a venal and corrupt elite that sharpens the various divisions that already exist. Just as the NLD rejected and boycotted the reform process in the early 2000s as mere entrenchment of military political power, the ethnic leaders may similarly abandon the political process altogether. The endogenous and exogenous factors are now largely favourable to withdrawal. Only the ethnic nationalities question now stands in their way. By conducting the political process on their terms, the *Tatmadaw* is ensuring that opposition politics is robbed of the political space with which to address the ethnic nationalities head on. The NLD is now the only group that has the cultural and political capacity to do this. In its continuous failure to do so it may yet plunge Myanmar into a period of political instability once again.

Bibliography

Al Jazeera. "Kachin rebels say Myanmar ignoring ceasefire." *Al Jazeera*, 21/2/2013, http://www.aljazeera.com/news/asia-pacific/2013/01/20131212566922246.html, (Accessed: 26/2/2013)

Alagappa, Muthiah. *Asian Security Practice : Material and Ideational Influences*. Palo Alto: Stanford University Press, 1998. Book.

———. *Coercion and Governance: The Declining Political Role of the Military in Asia*. Palo Alto: Stanford University Press, 2001.

Anderson, Benedict. *Imagined communities: Reflections on the origin and spread of nationalism*. London: Verso, 1991.

Aspinall, E., and M. Mietzner. *Problems of Democratisation in Indonesia: Elections, Institutions, and Society*. Singapore: Institute of Southeast Asian Studies, 2010.

"Aung San Suu Kyi tells of fondness for Burma army." *BBC News*, 27/01/2013, http://www.bbc.co.uk/news/uk-21217884, (Accessed: 10/02/2013)

Aye Aye Win. "Myanmar general defends military's political role." *Associated Press*, 27/3/2012, http://www.guardian.co.uk/world/feedarticle/10165291, (Accessed: 8/01/2013)

Baldwin, David A. "The concept of security." *Review of International Studies* 23, no. 1 (1997): 5-26.

Barta, Patrick. "Final Frontier: Firms Flock to Newly Opened Myanmar." *The Wall Street Journal*, http://online.wsj.com/article/SB10000872396390443749204578050773460553586.html, (Accessed: 02/02/2013)

BBC HARDtalk. "BBC HARDtalk Interview - U Thein Sein - President of Burma [VIDEO]." 8/1/2013, http://www.youtube.com/watch?v=7dP6ohVYYAg, (Accessed: 1/02/2013)

Beeson, Mark, and Alex J Bellamy. *Securing Southeast Asia*. London: Routledge, 2007.

Bertrand, J. *Nationalism and Ethnic Conflict in Indonesia*. Cambridge: Cambridge University Press, 2004.

Brand, Marcus. "'A bird in the hand...' The federal pattern of Myanmar's 2008 Constitution." Unpublished work. Used with author's permission, 2012.

Brandon, John J. *Burma/Myanmar Towards the Twenty-First Century: The Dynamics of Continuity and Change*. New York: Open Society Institute, 1997.

Brown, D. *The State and Ethnic Politics in South-East Asia*. London: Routledge, 1994.

Bünte, Marco. "Burma's transition to "disciplined democracy": Abdication or institutionalization of military rule?": GIGA working papers, 2011.

"Burma dam: Work halted on divisive Myitsone project." *BBC News*, http://www.bbc.co.uk/news/world-asia-pacific-15121801, (Accessed: 5/1/2013)

Callahan, Mary. "The Endurance of Military Rule in Burma: Not Why, But Why Not?'." (2010).

———. "The Generals Loosen Their Grip." *Journal of Democracy* 23, no. 4 (2012): 120-31.

———. *Making Enemies: War and State Building in Burma*. Ithaca, N.Y.: Cornell University Press, 2003.

Carey, P.B.R. *Burma: The Challenge of Change in a Divided Society*. MacMilan, St. Martin's Press, 1997.

Chan, Paul Chi-yuen, and Simon Shen. "Challenging the Transitoligist Approach: Myanmar's Troubled Democratization." In *Public Governance in Asia and the Limits of Electoral Democracy* edited by B. Bridges and Lock S. Ho. Cheltenham, UK: Edward Elgar Publishing, 2010.

Collier, David, and Steven Levitsky. "Democracy with Adjectives: Conceptual Innovation in Comparative Research." *World Politics* 49, no. 03 (1997): 430-51.

Croissant, Aurel. "Riding the tiger: civilian control and the military in democratizing Korea." *Armed Forces & Society* 30, no. 3 (2004): 357-81.

Croissant, Aurel, and Marco Bünte. *The Crisis of Democratic Governance in Southeast Asia*. Basingstoke: Palgrave Macmillan, 2011.

Croissant, Aurel, Paul W. Chambers, and Philip Völkel. "Democracy, the Military and Security Sector Governance in Indonesia, the Philippines and Thailand." In *The Crisis of Democratic Governance in Southeast Asia*, edited by A. Croissant and M. Bünte. 190-208. Basingstoke: Palgrave Macmillan, 2011.

Croissant, Aurel, and David Kuehn. "Civilian Control of the Military and Democracy: Conceptual and Theoretical Perspectives." In *Democracy under Stress: Civil-Military Relations in South and Southeast Asia*, edited by Paul Chambers and Aurel Croissant. Bangkok: ISIS, 2010.

Crouch, H.A. *Political Reform in Indonesia After Soeharto*. Singapore: Institute of Southeast Asian Studies, 2010.

Dahl, R.A. *Polyarchy: Participation & Opposition*. New Haven: Yale University Press, 1971.

Diamond, Larry. *Developing Democracy: Toward Consolidation*. Baltimore: Johns Hopkins University Press, 1999.

Diamond, Larry J., and Doh Chull Shin. *Institutional Reform and Democratic Consolidation in Korea*. Washington, D.C.: Hoover Inst. Press, 1999.

Diamond, Larry Jay. "Thinking about hybrid regimes." *Journal of Democracy* 13, no. 2 (2002): 21-35.

Dittmer, Lowell. "Burma vs. Myanmar: What's in a Name?". *Asian Survey* 48, no. 6 (2008): 885-88.

Fink, Christina. "Militarization in Burma's ethnic states: causes and consequences." *Contemporary Politics* 14, no. 4 (2008/12/01 2008): 447-62.

Foundation, Heritage. "Burma." *2013 Index of Economic Freedom*, http://www.heritage.org/index/country/burma, (Accessed: 27/02/2013)

Freedom House. "Burma Report." In *Freedom in the World Index*: Freedom House, 2013.

Fuller, Thomas. "In Public Eye, Shining Star of Myanmar Loses Luster." *The New York Times*, 09/03/2013, http://www.nytimes.com/2013/03/10/world/asia/in-public-eye-shining-star-of-myanmar-loses-luster.html, (Accessed: 9/03/2013)

Fundamental Principles and Detailed Basic Principles adopted by the National Convention in drafting the State Constitution. Naypyitaw: Printing and Publishing Enterprise, 2007. (Accessed.)

Geller, Martinne. "Coke ships first drinks to Myanmar in decades." *Reuters*, 10/09/2012, http://www.reuters.com/article/2012/09/10/us-cocacola-myanmar-idUSBRE8890MW20120910, (Accessed: 15/12/2012)

Ghai, Y.P., and J. Cottrell. *The Millennium Declaration, Rights, And Constitutions*. New Delhi: Oxford University Press, 2011.

Goddard, Geoffrey. "Ministry, UN launch project for first Myanmar census in 30 years." *The Myanmar Times*, http://www.mmtimes.com/index.php/national-news/yangon/3606-ministry-un-launch-project-for-first-myanmar-census-in-30-years.html, (Accessed: 5/1/2013)

Government of Myanmar. *Constitution of the Republic of the Union of Myanmar.* Naypyitaw: Ministry of Information, 2008. http://www.burmalibrary.org/docs5/Myanmar_Constitution-2008-en.pdf. (Accessed: 15/01/2013.)

"Govt property auction nets K800b." *The Myanmar Times*, http://www.mmtimes.com/index.php/national-news/yangon/3606-ministry-un-launch-project-for-first-myanmar-census-in-30-years.html, (Accessed: 5/1/2013)

Hlaing, Kyaw Yin. "Power and factional struggles in post-independence Burmese governments." *Journal of Southeast Asian Studies* 39, no. 01 (2008): 149-77.

―――. "Setting the rules for survival: why the Burmese military regime survives in an age of democratization." *The Pacific Review* 22, no. 3 (2009/08/06 2009): 271-91.

―――. "Understanding Recent Political Changes in Myanmar." *Contemporary Southeast Asia: A Journal of International and Strategic Affairs* 34, no. 2 (2012): 197-216.

Holliday, Ian. *Burma Redux: Global Justice and the Quest for Political Reform in Myanmar.* New York: Columbia University Press, 2012.

―――. "Ethnicity and Democratization in Myanmar." *Asian Journal of Political Science* 18, no. 2 (2010): 111-28.

Huntington, S.P. *The Soldier and the State: The Theory and Politics of Civil-Military Relations.* Cambridge: Harvard University Press, 1957.

ICG (International Crisis Group). "Myanmar's Post-Election Landscape." *Crisis Group Asia Briefing*, no. 118, March (2011).

―――. "Reform in Myanmar: One Year On." *Crisis Group Asia Briefing*, no. 136, April (2012).

Khiang, Mi Mi. "Burmese Names: A guide." *The Atlantic*, 1958.

Koh, K.S. *Misunderstood Myanmar: An Introspective Study of a Southeast Asian State in Transition.* Singapore: Humanities Press, 2011.

Kohn, Richard H. "How democracies control the military." *Journal of Democracy* 8, no. 4 (1997): 140-53.

Lawson, Stephanie. "Conceptual Issues in the Comparative Study of Regime Change and Democratization." *Comparative politics* 25, no. 2 (1993): 183-205.

Levitsky, Steven, and Lucan Way. "The rise of competitive authoritarianism." *Journal of Democracy* 13, no. 2 (2002): 51-65.

"Mass rally supports seven-point roadmap clarified by Prime Minister." *The New Light of Myanmar*, 20/09/2003, http://www.ibiblio.org/obl/docs/rallies-etc..htm, (Accessed: 07/01/2013)

McCartan, Brian. "Land grabbing as big business in Myanmar." *Asia Times Online*, 8/03/2013, http://www.atimes.com/atimes/Southeast_Asia/SEA-01-080313.html, (Accessed: 10/03/2013)

"Myanmar formally announces ratification of new constitution draft." *People's Daily Online*, 30/05/2008, http://english.people.com.cn/90001/90777/90851/6421254.html, (Accessed: 14/01/2013)

Nordlinger, Eric A. *Soldiers in politics: military coups and governments.* London: Prentice-Hall, 1977.

O'Donnell, G.A. *Dissonances: democratic critiques of democracy.* Notre Dame, IN: University of Notre Dame Press, 2007.

O'Donnell, Guillermo, Philippe C Schmitter, and Laurence Whitehead. *Transitions from authoritarian rule: comparative perspectives.* Vol. 4, London: Johns Hopkins University Press, 1986.

Oommen, T.K. *Citizenship and national identity: from colonialism to globalism.* London: Sage Publications, 1997.

Oppenheimer, Michael F. "From Prediction to Recognition: Using Alternate Scenarios to Improve Foreign Policy Decisions." *SAIS Review* 32, no. 1 (2012): 19-31.

Pace, Julie. "Obama makes history with Myanmar, Cambodia visits." *Associated Press,* 20/11/2012, http://bigstory.ap.org/article/obama-myanmar-show-power-new-beginning, (Accessed: 07/02/2013)

Pedersen, Morten B. "The Politics of Burma's "Democratic" Transition." *Critical Asian Studies* 43, no. 1 (2011): 49-68.

Putnam, R.D., R. Leonardi, and Rafaella Y. Nanetti. *Making Democracy Work: Civic Traditions in Modern Italy.* Princeton, N.J.: Princeton University Press, 1993.

Rustow, Dankwart A. "Transitions to democracy: Toward a dynamic model." *Comparative politics* 2, no. 3 (1970): 337-63.

Schneider, Carsten Q, and Philippe C Schmitter. "Liberalization, transition and consolidation: measuring the components of democratization." *Democratization* 11, no. 5 (2004): 59-90.

Schumpeter, Joseph A. *Capitalism, Socialism, and Democracy.* London: Harper Perennial Modern Classics, 2008. 1975.

Selth, A. *Burma's armed forces: power without glory.* Norwalk, Conn.: EastBridge, 2002.

Singh, B. *Civil-military relations in democratising Indonesia: the potentials and limits to change.* Canberra: Strategic and Defence Studies Centre, Australian National University, 2001.

Smith, Alan. "Ethnicity and federal prospect in Myanmar." Chap. 9 In *Federalism in Asia,* edited by B. He, B. Galligan and T. Inoguchi. 188-212. Cheltenham: Edward Elgar, 2009.

Stepan, Alfred, Juan J Linz, and Yogendra Yadav. *Crafting State-Nations: India and other multinational democracies.* Baltimore: Johns Hopkins University Press, 2011.

Taylor, R.H. *The State in Myanmar.* London: C Hurst & Co Publishers Ltd, 2009.

Taylor, Robert. "Myanmar: military politics and the prospects for democratisation." *Asian Affairs* 29, no. 1 (1998/03/01 1998): 3-12.

Terwiel, B. J. *Thailand's Political History: From the 13th Century to Recent Times.* Bangkok: River Books, 2011.

Than, M. "Myanmar: Preoccupation with Regime Survival, National Unity and Stability." In *Asian Security Practice: Material and Ideational Influences,* edited by M. Alagappa. Palo Alto: Stanford University Press, 1998.

Thant Myint-U. *The River of Lost Footsteps: Histories of Burma.* London: Faber and Faber, 2007.

———. *Where China Meets India: Burma and the New Crossroads of Asia.* London: Faber & Faber, 2011.

Thawnghmung, Ardeth Maung. "Beyond armed resistance: ethnonational politics in Burma (Myanmar)." In *Policy Studies,* 67. Honolulu: East-West Center, 2011.

The Ministry of Foreign Affairs Website. "About Myanmar: Population." 2013.

Thu, Kyaw. "Suu Kyi Seeks Closer Army Ties After Re-Election as Party Leader." *Businessweek,* 10/03/2013, http://www.businessweek.com/news/2013-03-10/myanmar-s-opposition-party-elects-aung-san-suu-kyi-as-chairwoman, (Accessed: 10/03/2013)

Tun, Aung Hla. "Myanmar president promotes reformers in cabinet shake-up." *Reuters*, 27/08/2012, http://www.reuters.com/article/2012/08/27/us-myanmar-politics-idUSBRE87Q0QG20120827, (Accessed: 08/02/2013)

———. "Myanmar rebels say army ignoring president's ceasefire." *Reuters*, 20/02/2013, http://www.reuters.com/article/2013/01/20/us-myanmar-kachin-idUSBRE90J03820130120, (Accessed: 03/02/2013)

Tun, S.K.M. *State-Building in Myanmar (1988-2010) and Suharto's Indonesia: A Study of Building a Democratic Developmental State in Myanmar.* Saarbrucken, Germany: Lambert Academic Publishing, 2012.

Turnell, Sean. "Myanmar in 2011." *Asian Survey* 52, no. 1 (2012): 157-64.

Walton, Matthew J. "Ethnicity, conflict, and history in Burma: The myths of Panglong." *Asian Survey* 48, no. 6 (2008): 889-910.

Watts, Ronald L. *Comparing federal systems in the 1990s.* Kingston, Ont.: Institute of Intergovernmental Relations, Queen's University, 1996.

Zarni, Muang. "An Insider View of Reconciliation." In *Myanmar/Burma: Inside Challenges, Outside Interests*, edited by L. Rieffel. Washington, D.C.: Brookings Institution Press, 2010.

NLD Party Chairman, founding member and former journalist, U Win Tin, receives gifts from NLD members on the 4th anniversary of his release from prison. In 1989 Win Tin was arrested for his writings and NLD affiliation and spent the following 19 years in prison.
Downtown Yangon, 23/09/2012

NLD leaders gather for speeches on 4th anniversary of U Win Tin's release. Second from left U Win Tin. 3rd from left former general, commander-of-the-armed-forces, and Deputy Leader of the NLD, U Tin Oo
Downtown Yangon, 23/09/2012

Activists gather at NLD rally in Yangon for speeches by Deputy Leader U Tin Oo and Party Chairman U Win Tin.
Downtown Yangon, 23/09/2012

On the day of its re-entry into the country, Coca-Cola advert marks the company's first presence in the country in more the 60 years.
Yangon International Airport, 21/09/2012

All photographs author's own